BREAD *Cookies*

3

Add the molasses and
egg, and stir again.

4

Mix the flour, baking soda,
ginger, and salt in
a separate bowl.

7

Bake for 8–10 minutes,
depending on how thick
your cookies are and
whether you want them
chewy or crispy.

8

After the cookies cool,
decorate them with
icing if you like.

GINGERBREAD FOR LIBERTY!

How a
German Baker
Helped Win the
American Revolution

MARA ROCKLIFF

Pictures by

VINCENT X. KIRSCH

HOUGHTON MIFFLIN HARCOURT
Boston   New York

For my sister Consuelo,
who is always ready to feed an army.
—M.R.

To Paul,
who bakes with love.
—V.X.K.

www.hmhco.com

The text of this book is set in Cheltenham.
The illustrations were created using 140-lb. hot press watercolor paper, watercolor, and rubbelkrepp (masking fluid).

Library of Congress Cataloging-in-Publication Data is on file.

ISBN 978-0-544-13001-2

Manufactured in China
SCP 10 9 8 7 6 5 4 3 2 1
4500499378

Everyone in Philadelphia knew the gingerbread baker.
His honest face . . . his booming laugh . . .

And, of course, his gingerbread—the best in all the thirteen colonies. His big, floury hands turned out castles and queens, horses and cows and hens—each detail drawn in sweet, buttery icing with the greatest skill and care.

And yet, despite his care, there always seemed to be some broken pieces for the hungry children who followed their noses to the spicy-smelling shop.

"No empty bellies here!" the baker bellowed. "Not in *my* America!"

For once upon a time, he had been young and hungry too.
And he had followed his own nose to this New World, where
a hard-working young man could open his own bakery
and always have enough to eat.

But now, something was in the air (besides the smell of baking gingerbread).
Newspapers shouted

REVOLUTION!

INDEPENDENCE!

LIBERTY!

Boys rolled up blankets, shouldered guns, and kissed mothers goodbye.

The baker hung his apron up. He dusted flour off his hands.

"Where are you going?" asked his wife.

"To fight for my America!" he said. "I was a soldier once."

"That was long ago and far away," she said. "You are a baker now, and you are old and fat."

The baker knew his wife was right.
But he knew also that he loved his country.
Somehow, he had to find a way to help.

He packed his bags and went to join General Washington.

General Washington did not say the baker was
old and fat. General Washington was too polite.
Anyway, he had other troubles on his mind.

The baker rolled up his sleeves.
"No empty bellies here," he told General Washington. "Not in *my* America!"

But bigger trouble was on the way.

Across the ocean . . .

The king of England wrote to other rulers and hired THEIR armies to help him squash the revolution.

When the ships sailed into sight, even General Washington turned pale. Who had ever seen such an army?

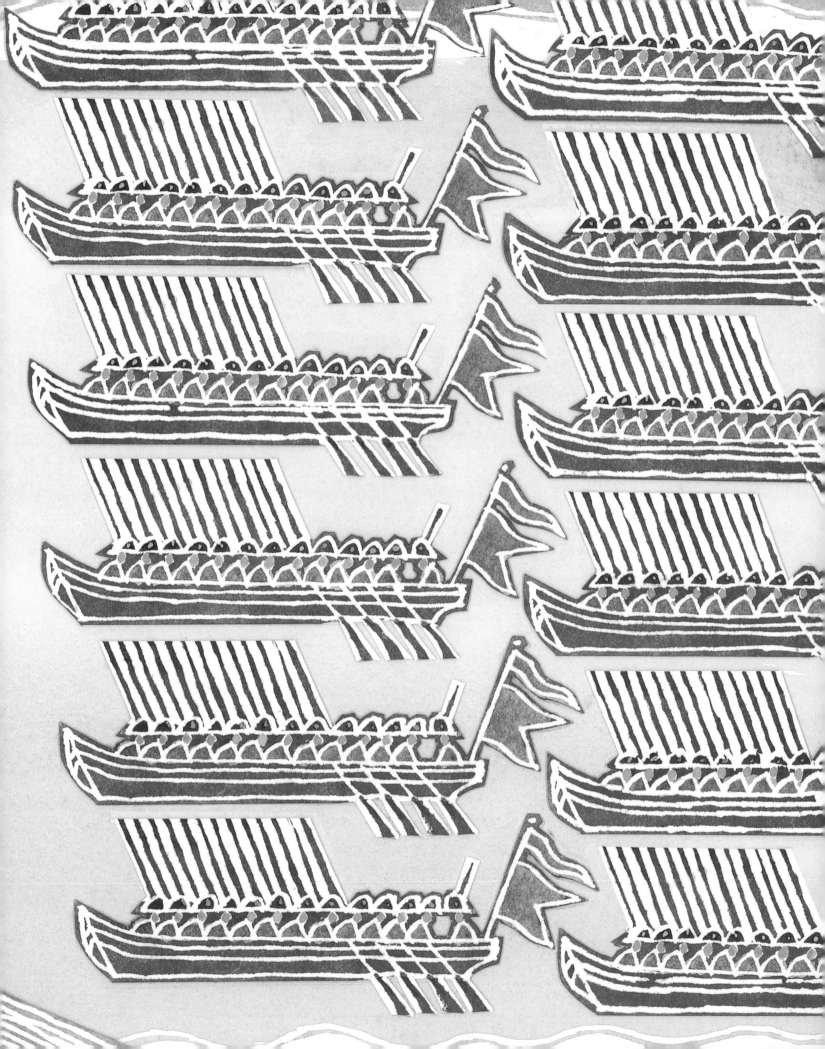

"These soldiers come from the land where I was born,"
the baker told General Washington. "Let me go speak to them.
Perhaps I can persuade them we are not their enemies.
Perhaps I can even persuade them to switch sides!"

"If you are caught, you will be killed," Washington warned.
The baker smiled. "Then I must not be caught."

In the darkest hour of the night, he rowed across the bay. With each dip of his oars, he thought of words to win the soldiers over to the American cause.

REVOLUTION! *(splash)*
Befreiung!

INDEPENDENCE! *(splash)*
Unabhängigkeit!

LIBERTY! *(splash, splash)*

Freiheit!

But when he looked into their hungry faces, all his fine words
slipped away.

What could he say?

"I have a bakeshop . . ." he began.

As the baker spoke, the soldiers seemed to see the fragrant steam rising from his ovens. They could almost smell the spicy gingerbread, and taste the sweet, buttery icing on their tongues.

"And you always have enough to eat?" the soldiers asked.

"No empty bellies here," the baker told them. "Not in *my* America!"

Across the ocean . . .

Many, many loaves—and battles!—later . . .

THE BRITISH HAVE SURRENDERED!
THE REVOLUTION IS OVER!
WE WON!

"My work is done!"
the baker cried.

Washington said, "Not quite."

A gift from General Washington

Did he bake the British soldiers gingerbread for their dessert?

We'll never know . . .

and his baker

They didn't leave a crumb.

Simple GINGER

Christopher Ludwick pressed his gingerbread dough into carved wooden molds. You can roll out your dough and cut it into shapes with cookie cutters. Or just use your fingers.

Ingredients

- 1 stick butter (softened)
- ½ cup sugar
- ½ cup molasses
- 1 egg
- 2½ cups flour
- 1 teaspoon baking soda
- 2 teaspoons ground ginger
- ½ teaspoon salt

1

Preheat your oven to 350°F.

2

Put the soft butter and sugar in a bowl and stir them with a fork.

5

Pour the dry mix into the wet mix and stir until you have a nice brown dough.

6

Form the dough into shapes and lay them on an ungreased cookie sheet.